You Are The Song

Inspired Writings
By
Sandra J Yearman

SERAPHIM PUBLISHING LLC

WE WILL BRING LIGHT TO ALL THE DARK PLACES

Registered trademark-
Sandra J Yearman
Seraphim Publishing
438 Water St. Cambridge, WI 53523

Copyright © 2008 Sandra J Yearman
Produced in the United States of America
Author : Sandra J Yearman
Editor: Sandra J Yearman
Cover Design by Sandra J Yearman
Layout and design by Sandra J Yearman

All rights reserved. No part of this book may be reproduced, stored in or introduced into a retrieval system, or transmitted, in any form or by any means, electronic or mechanical, including photocopying or recording or otherwise copied for public or private use—other than for "fair use" as brief quotations embodied in articles and reviews–without written permission from the author.

Library of Congress Control Number: 2009906248
ISBN: 978-0-9815791-6-0
First Edition

To
God
Of All The Worlds That Ever Were
Of All The Worlds That Ever Will Be
Of All Times And Of All Ages
Of All Creation
Amen
Amen
Amen

CONTENTS

DEDICATION

You Are The Song..7
He Called My Name..9
The Warrior With White Wings........................11
God Will Send Me Sunshine.............................13
Hand Of God 17
Clarity 19
Gifts..21
God Hold My Hand..23
The Birth Of The King.....................................25
God...28
I Surrender...29
Presence...30
Until The End Of Days.....................................32
Little Lamb...35
Perception..37

SEEKING LIGHT IN THE DARKNESS

Lift Us Out Of Darkness...................................41
Lord, I Crawl To Your Feet..............................43
To Dream...45
Do You Hear Me..49
Lord I am Broken...51

CONTENTS

War..53
We Cry For Ourselves And Each Other...........56
God, Do We Make You Cry...............................58
God Please Save Creation..................................61
He Has Won..64

COMING HOME

Awaken..67
Battlefields Of Hope..69
Lord Cleanse Us From The Darkness 71
I Will Lead You Home......................................73
The Christmas Gift..77
Trumpets Of The Angels...................................81
I Set A Place For Jesus 83
One Flame...85
A Love Song For Our King...............................87

Dedication

You Are The Song

I heard a Song
It was like no other

The melody was familiar
But I had forgotten the sound

The Song filled my being
And brought life to my heart

The Song cleansed me
The Song healed me

The Song gave me faith
And strength
And purpose

The Song brought me comfort
The Song brought me peace
The Song blessed me

God You are the Song that my soul sings

God You are the Song that gives life to my being

God You are the Song that consumes me

God You are the Song of my life

Amen Amen Amen

He Called My Name

He called my name
And I listened

It was just a whisper
And it filled my being

He fed my soul
He nourished my body

He is my shield
He is my sword

He teaches me
He loves me
He blesses me

He changed my life
And I never looked back

God, I love You
Fill me with Your Being
Engulf me with the Holiness of Your Spirit

Show me the path You would have for me
Guide me
Give me what I need to do Thy Will

Amen Amen Amen

The Warrior With White Wings

Darkness shrieks with horror
As God's Light takes the battlefield
The armies of the darkness
Crumble, fall and yield

The Warrior with the white wings
Took God's Holy Stand
He stood on the battlefield
Before every woman, child and man

The Son, God sent with Mercy
The Warrior sent with Love
The Savior of His children
The Father from above

The blessed men of Holiness
Who, with Holy hearts
Stood before their Lord
And refuse to succumb to the dark

The Warrior with the white wings
Took God's Holy Stand
He stood on the battlefield
Before every woman, child and man

The battle wages always
For creations life
God sent His Holy Son
To save us from this strife

In these days of darkness
Let us never be afraid to pray
And ask the Holy Savior
To make a brighter day

Amen Amen Amen

God Will Send Me Sunshine

When this journey is more than I can bear
With anguish I do cry
Overwhelmed I am with pain
And my spirit is ready to die

For in this world of darkness
In sin and pain I have roamed
But, I believe God will send me sunshine
To show me my way Home

When my shoulders can no longer carry
The burdens of my life
When my spirit is so broken
I can no longer bear this way of strife

For in this world of darkness
In sin and pain I have roamed
But, I believe God will send me sunshine
To show me my way Home

When friends they have forsaken
And wearily I crawl
Death would be a blessing
I have been betrayed by them all

For in this world of darkness
In sin and pain I have roamed
But, I believe God will send me sunshine
To show me my way Home

This world it is a challenge
Sometimes I followed its dark ways
Lord lift me from this nightmare
Now on my knees I do pray

For in this world of darkness
In sin and pain I have roamed
But, I believe God will send me sunshine
To show me my way Home

Lord my faith at times has varied
And often I have lost my way
And through this cloud of darkness
For forgiveness I do pray

For in this world of darkness
In sin and pain I have roamed
But, I believe God will send me sunshine
To show me my way Home

Lord, I believe You will show me mercy
Even when I have gone a stray
Lord my faith You will carry
And Your Glory I will witness one day

For in this world of darkness
In sin and pain I have roamed
But, I believe God will send me sunshine
To show me my way Home

Amen Amen Amen

Hand Of God

My heart is filled with mercy
For those I have not seen
For the animals that dwell with us
In Holy company

My arms can shelter many
With God's help I will be strong
To stand before the victims
To right what has been wronged

My voice can cry to Heaven
For many more than me
And I know God will listen
My faith abounds in Thee

My time here is not lengthy
I pray God, that it is spent
Working as a hand of God
Wherever I am sent

Amen Amen Amen

Clarity

The teachers are not to be worshipped
It is the message that they bring
The children are crying in the darkness
Looking for the Holy Spring

The children in their anguish
Often fail to see
That anyone can speak with God
The warrior on his knees

Jesus with His sacrifice
Set our souls free
He did not distinguish
With His Holy Mercy

Teachers should be messengers
Not obstacles to block the Son
God loves His children
And cares for everyone

You need no special passage
No documents or degrees
To cry out to the Heavens
To pray upon your knees

Amen Amen Amen

Gifts

He asked me
"Do you pray"
"I speak with God"
"Most every day"

I looked at Him
In my night
And through my tears
I said, "Not as I might"

As I listened
To what He said
I chose to change
I chose not to walk among the dead

When I left
That Holy man
I felt like God
Had taken my hand

As I wander
As I seek
I share my gifts
With those I meet

And when the Spirit
Carries me
I spread the Light
I was allowed to see

When I encounter a soul
Who is walking in the night
Who is consumed with fear
With terror and fright

I ask him
"Do you pray"
"I speak with God"
"Most every day"

Amen Amen Amen

God Hold My Hand

God hold my hand
And steady me in these turbulent times

God hold my hand
And comfort me when I am scared

God hold my hand
And whisper to me when I need a friend

God hold my hand
And guide me when I am lost

God hold my hand
And we will soar

God hold my hand
And take me home

Amen Amen Amen

The Birth Of The King

His birth stopped time in our world
Heaven and earth were aligned
Galaxies of Angels sang in praise

The Holiest of Songs
The Song of God Himself

God blessed our world and mankind
The Song was a whisper
The Song grew to a roar

The Holy King was born
The King was surrounded first, with
the creations of God

The stars danced in the skies
And their light announced the most
Blessed of Miracles

That God had sent a King
To bring Light to the darkness
To bring His Holy message
To bring this world, filled with darkness, closer to Heaven

The King brought God's Love
The King brought God's Message
The King held a mirror to our darkness
The King showed us the path to God's Light

The King walked among us as a man
The King stood before us as our God

Thank You, Heavenly Father,
For the most extraordinary, majestic
And Holy Gift our world has ever received

Your Love
Your Son
Our King

Amen Amen Amen

God

God You are the substance of my soul
The nourishment of my being
You are the passion of my heart

God You are my song
You are my strength
You are my blessing
You are my Light in these dark times

Lord God You are my Heavenly Father
My spirit flies, I am free
Of the bonds and chains of this world

Amen Amen Amen

I Surrender

God Your Presence overwhelms me
Your Song carries me above this world
Your Love saturates me

I will sing Your Song forever
I will worship only You
I will surrender
My life, my heart, my soul to You alone
My God

Amen Amen Amen

Presence

Lord thank You for Your Presence
Thank You for Your Love
Thank You for Your Grace
You bless us from above

Lord thank You for the radiance
Of the Light You send our way
Thank You for the Angels
Who watch us every day

Lord thank You for our blessings
From our Savior most high
Who redeems us with His Life
So we will never die

Lord thank You for Your Word
That guides us every day
And thank You for the Promises
Of a life that we may

Live without torment
Live without fear
Be healed from our frailties
And have You hold us near

Amen Amen Amen

Until The End Of Days

When darkness over takes me
And in the chaos I go astray
When I am blind and I am injured
And to my death I lay

I will call upon You, Lord
And ask to be shown the Way
And I will sing You love songs
Until the end of days

When I stumble and I fall
From the burdens of this life
When I lose my self in the darkness
When I am filled with strife

I will call upon You, Lord
And ask to be shown the Way
And I will sing You love songs
Until the end of days

When weary from the torment
And the hatred that I wear
When this world of chaos
Is more than I can bear

I will call upon You, Lord
And ask to be shown the Way
And I will sing You love songs
Until the end of days

When my breath is fading
And my body yearns to sleep
When the frailties of this life
My strength no longer keeps

I will call unto You, Lord
And ask to be shown the Way
And I will sing You love songs
Until the end of days

When my heart stops beating
And my spirit is set free
When my God comes for me
And I will truly see

I will sing You love songs
Until the end of days

Amen Amen Amen

Little Lamb

Hang on to these words
My little lamb
Until He comes
The Great I AM

Pray to God
With all your might
He will save you from the darkness
He will save you from the night

Do not fear
His words to read
Or to emulate
His Holy deeds

For God is with us
One and all
He is only waiting
For you to call

Upon His Name
Through His Son
The battle still raging
But the war is won

Hang on to these words
My little lamb
Until He comes
The Great I AM

Amen Amen Amen

Perception

I cried out in my darkness
As I believed my world was filled with pain
Then I looked around me
And my humility did gain

The crosses that I was bearing
Were small indeed
In this world of destruction
In this world of horror and need

I was so blind to others
That I did not realize
That seeing through the darkness
Was my unholy guise

I can eat when I am hungry
I can pray without fear
I have clothes for my body
I have much that I hold dear

As I looked into my soul
I began to realize
That I had been looking at my life
With unholy eyes

My house may be modest
But it is a loving home
Filled with family and friends
I would not want to roam

I have arms to hold my loved ones
I have legs to run the race
Eyes to see the beauty
Of wonders, I do taste

I have the freedom to make choices
To think as I would choose
I have a life without barriers
My freedoms I would not want to lose

Perception is a blessing
Which I had failed to understand
I allowed myself to submerge in darkness
In this world of man

Lord, thank You for my blessings
And please allow me to see
That my life is filled with miracles
And many blessings sent from Thee.

Amen Amen Amen

Seeking Light In The Darkness

Lift Us Out Of Darkness

God we beg of You to pardon us for our sins
Lift us out of the darkness and into Your Light
Engulf us with Your Love
Guide us and protect us
Show us the path You would have us take

Fill us with Your Grace
Help us to understand
Ignite within us the Flame of the Holy Spirit
We surrender to Your Holiness

Let us dwell in the House of the Lord
Let the Lord dwell in our homes and in our hearts
Teach us, oh Lord to pray

Help us to remember the Holiness in which we were created
Help us to see the Holiness in all of Your creations

Bless us and carry us this day

Amen Amen Amen

Lord I Crawl To Your Feet

Lord I crawl to Your feet
I have been so long from Your
Presence
I am dying
I am dead

My sins have overwhelmed me
I feel no life
I feel no love
I feel only pain and anguish

I am walking the path of the dead
I feel nothing
Others can not see the pain I am in
Others do not see me

Lord, am I invisible to You also
I am numbed by the horror that I have
witnessed

I am pierced by the terror I have seen
I have lost so much
I have lost myself

Lord can You see me
Lord can You hear me
Lord can You forgive me

Lord I need You, yet I am so lifeless I can barely speak
Teach me the words, God
Breathe life back into me

Fill me with Your Holiness
Rescue me

Amen Amen Amen

To Dream

I drew a picture
For all to see
Of the different worlds
That had appeared to me

And in this dream
I did not understand
The world I saw
That belonged to man

I heard the screams
I heard them cry
I felt their terror
I saw them die

The walls they built
To separate
To hide in fear
To perpetuate hate

Another world
I was allowed to see
Was very different
From the one in front of me

It was as warm
As the Son
A world without boundaries
A world worshipping One

These worlds were so near
As to touch
But the fear was great
The hatred much

The Light and the Spirit
Tried to enter in
But the world of man
Could not hear through the din

The Voice I heard
Was soft and strong
"Come my children"
"I will correct the wrongs"

But as I watched
The world of man
Less and less
Could I understand

They chose not to listen
They chose to seal the gate
They chose the cold darkness
The terror and hate

I tried to scream out
In my fright
"Do you understand what you are doing"
"You are choosing the night"

The Voice I heard
Was soft and strong
"Come my children"
"I will correct the wrongs"

Amen Amen Amen

Do You Hear Me

Lord God I cry out in pain
Do You hear me
My voice is weak
I weep, yet, my face is dry
My tears have dried up long ago

I mourn the death of my soul
I mourn the death of one I love
I do not understand

God help me to understand
Help me to endure
Help me to live again
Help me to love again

Lord I cry out in anguish
I cry
I cry

Please God listen to my pleas
Help me oh God, help me oh God
Have mercy upon me

I do not understand death
I do not understand loss
I do not understand

Save me with Your redeeming Grace
Lift me up
Carry me
Heal me

Give me strength
Give me faith
Give me life

Amen Amen Amen

Lord I Am Broken

Lord it has been so long since I have prayed
Please forgive me

Lord I am broken and I can not fix my life
I am lost and I can not find my way
I am dead yet I linger

Lord I am so weary
Please lift my crippled body out of the darkness
And carry me into the Light

Lord please breathe life back into me
And return me to the living

Lord please save me, I can not save myself
Lord please free me, I can not free myself

Amen Amen Amen

War

Lord the war is raging
The darkness is upon us

We hear the cries of terror
Blood flows like water
The bodies are distorted
Horror overwhelms us

We have lost our souls
We have lost all feelings
We have lost our will

We cry and we have no tears
We scream and there is no sound

We die we die we die
And the world watches

We die and no one helps
We die and we can not help ourselves

Lord please stand before us
Lord please breathe life back into us
Lord please restore our souls

Lord God cleanse the filth and decay from our bodies
Lord God heal our wounds
Lord God restore our souls

Lord God rescue us from this place of hell
Lord God carry us

Lord God fill us with the Holy Spirit
And restore us to the Holy vessels You created

Lord God fill us and our world
With Your Grace
With Your Peace
With Your Love

Amen Amen Amen

We Cry For Ourselves And Each Other

We cry, we cry, we cry
We feel so alone
As darkness surrounds us

We hear other voices crying
But we can not see through our own pain
We hear the cries for help
But our broken limbs can not move

Lord are we dead
Lord are we alone
Lord we are so lost

Lord send us a Light in the darkness
Lord calm our fears
Lord save us and stand before us

Lord forgive us
Forgive us
Forgive us

Amen Amen Amen

God Do We Make You Cry

Lord God Holy Savior
Of all the worlds that ever were
Of all the worlds that ever will be
Of all times and of all ages
Of all creation

God do we ever make You cry

Do we hurt You with the ways we
defile the gifts You give us
Do we horrify You with the ways we
call darkness into our souls
Into our lives, into our worlds

Do we shame You with our false gods
Our false prophets
Our greed and our violence

Do we anger You when we spread our
darkness to all of Your creation
When we destroy entire species
When we destroy entire cultures
When we stand by and let the
darkness consume this world

God do we ever make You cry

When we refuse to listen to Your Voice
When we refuse to feel Your Presence
When we refuse to believe
After all You have done for us

God forgive us
Lord God stop the murders, the holocausts, the exterminations
Lord Father stop the darkness

Lord Savior rescue us
Lord God save us

Amen Amen Amen

God Please Save Creation

'God bless you and your species'
The baby Angel said
The tears of Heaven flow
For the world of the walking dead

God bless your Maker
For putting you in our care
How does the face of man
Look to Heaven and dare

Make excuses...
For their murderous greed
To honor and save the preciousness of life
They refuse to see the need

In a world of rape and plunder
Where the victims are the bait
Where man worships money over life
And perpetuates terror and hate

And the baby Angel prayed to Heaven
'Lord, save the victims here'
'Break through this unholy darkness'
'Bring the Heavens near'

'Help mankind to understand'
'That life force is a gift'
'No matter how it is packaged'
'Heal these unholy rifts'

Animals have no voices
The plants, earth and the sky
We destroy all that sustains us
And the baby Angel asks 'Why'

'Can they not see the uniqueness in creation'
'The God- source in all life'
'How precious all creation is'
'How Holy is all life'

And as the baby Angel wept
For a world of dying decay
The God-Face of Christ smiled upon her
And said, 'We will help make a better way'

Amen Amen Amen

He Has Won

The demons kill with such disregard
Their victims show their status
Destruction and terror in their wake
What horror would await us

If we cower before them
In fear and in shame
The demons draw power
From their fearful games

But, the Light in the night
Fears no assault
For it is the Light of the Heavens
The God we exalt

Help is within us
His Name we must cry
Ask for God
To save you from the lies

Light dissolves darkness
It is the Holy task
Pray to the Heavens
For Salvation we must ask

The Shepherd stands before the sheep
The Father before the Son
Ask that God will fight your demons
A Holy war He has won

Amen Amen Amen

Coming Home

Awaken

Only the one dancing hears the Music
Only the one dancing hears the Song
Only the one dancing listens

To a melody from the Heavens
A Song so sweet and pure
A Song of faith and courage
A Song to draw God near

And the melody shall lift you
And the Song will make you soar
And the Music conquers darkness
And the words shall ever more

Change the way you see things
Take away your fears
Cleanse you from the darkness
Draw the Heavens near

Amen Amen Amen

Battlefields of Hope

The horses galloped
On the field
Where blood was shed
Where mankind yield

The fathers had told
Of a battle so great
The stories of old
Of a formidable hate

Worlds that were lost
Worlds that were saved
Of saints and of demons
Of a Father who gave

As old as the ages
As old as life
Mankind has choices
Between Heaven and strife

Worlds gone crazy
Some have atoned
Sons sold in battle
Souls searching for Home

Herald the Angels
Armies on wings
The Son and the Father
Of whom Heaven sings

Veils are removed
Awaken and see
God sent His Angels
His Christ Face of Three

To save all His children
To carry them Home
Lost on the battlefields
No more will they roam

Amen Amen Amen

Lord Cleanse Us From The Darkness

Our Dear Lord God forgive us all
Cleanse us from the darkness that cloaks us
Carry us this day

Lord God in Heaven engulf us in Your Holy Presence
Consume us with the Fire of Heaven
We surrender our hearts, our lives, our souls to You

Help us to understand Your Will
Help us to do Your Will to the best of our abilities
Let us hear Your Voice in the darkness
Dwell in our homes, in our hearts and in our very beings

Use us as instruments of Your Will
and tools of Your Hand

Bless us with Your Love, Your Grace
and Your Peace

Lord God let Your Will be done
Let Your Will be done

Amen Amen Amen

I Will Lead You Home

Wandering in these dark worlds
Weary from my roam
I cried out from the darkness
Weak and all alone

I heard an Angel whisper
Her Voice as sweet as a song
'Take hold of my hand '
'And I will lead you Home'

At first I doubted my sanity
For what could this really be
What was this voice I was hearing
What did I really see

'I have been watching you in the darkness'
'I cry for all your fears'
'Take hold of my hand'
'And I will bring the Heavens near'

The Angel cried out to Heaven
'Father forgive your children here'
'They flounder in the darkness'
'They fill their lives with fear'

'Who are you,' I asked the Angel
'And why are you here'
'I have been with you always'
'God keeps His children near'

'He has been waiting for you to request His Presence'
'He has been waiting for you to ask to hear His Voice'
'He created you with free will'
'Your path is of your own choice'

'You can choose to slay the demons'
'You can choose to live in fear'
'You can choose to have your freedom'
'You can call the Heavens near'

I listened to this Angel
Her voice as sweet as a Song
She said 'Your Holy Father will forgive you'
'And correct what is wrong'

I cried out in my darkness
I asked the Angel to stay
I prayed to God for forgiveness
I prayed for God to make a better Way

I heard an Angel whisper
Her Voice as sweet as a song
'Take hold of my hand'
'And I will lead you Home'

Amen Amen Amen

The Christmas Gift

The Christmas I remember most
Was inspired by the Holy Host
My family I did not see
I stayed with those preparing a journey
to Thee

Abandoned by many
Confined to their beds
Forgotten and lonely
Their lifetimes had lead

To a cancer ward
Busy and sterile
No songs, no laughter
No children to giggle

A friend and I
Volunteered to spend Christmas night
And the experiences we had
Filled us with Light

You see, the Angels walked
Down those long halls
They touched all the bodies
They answered the calls

Our spirits were lifted
We danced and we sang
And the Spirit of Christmas
Was felt by every woman and man

Though, their families had not gathered
God gave them great gifts
The Spirit of Love
From darkness did lift

We became one big family
That night
God healed their fears
God dissolved their fright

When the sun rose
In the sky
We did not want to leave
We questioned why

The Spirit of God
Did not consume us every day
We prayed and we prayed
For the Holy Spirit to stay

The best Christmas gift
I ever received
Was the night I spent caring
For those preparing a journey to Thee

Amen Amen Amen

Trumpets Of The Angels

Heaven rejoiced
As no time before
Jesus saved creation
From hell's dark door

The worlds were filled
With Love and Song
For God had fulfilled His promises
And corrected what was wrong

The Angels played Holy instruments
Music as this world has never heard
With wings of gold and trumpets
The Victory of God they herald

This Song will ring through eternity
This Holy Song has no end
For the Father saved His children
He saved the world of men

So that His children would never
forget their blessings
So that His children would never
forget the Victory
God gave us a symbol
A symbol of white to represent purity

This symbol is a flower
Delicate and strong
To represent the Angel's trumpets
To represent God's Song

This flower we call the lily
A symbol on Easter Day
That God saved His children
That God promised a better Way

Amen Amen Amen

I Set A Place For Jesus

Lord some people have altars in their homes
Some people remove You from their lives
Some people only call upon You
When they are crumbling under the weight of strife

How can we pray to a God
That we keep at such a distance
Do we only believe in You on Sundays
Or are You part of our existence

I pray to You everyday
But as much as I was able
That did not seem like enough
Until I set a place for You at my table

Although the gesture is quite simple
It reminds me everyday
That You are part of my life
Even when I choose to stray

Sometimes we need reminding
That God is always with us
I found I could remember
By this symbol as a witness

God has a place at my table
Each and every day
To remind me I am blessed
And that I need not stray

Amen Amen Amen

One Flame

One Flame flickered in the darkness
The Source to God was known
For into the world of man
God sent one of His own

To Light the path to Heaven
To expose the demon masks
To give hope to all God's children
Was the Holy task

To teach the Song of Heaven
To heal the heart and soul
To give a Voice to the victims
Was the Holy goal

The Flame dissolved the darkness
The Flame ignited creation
One Flame, the Gift of Heaven
Will remain through all duration

One Flame flickered in the darkness
The Source to God was known
For into the world of man
God sent one of His own

Amen Amen Amen

A Love Song For Our King

Lord, does anyone ever write You love songs
For all the world to see
Lord I have little to give
But here is a love song written by me

Thank You for my blessings
Thank You for my life
Thank You for carrying me
When I am overwhelmed with strife

Thank You for my family
And my friends galore
Thank You for the sunshine
And so very much more

But thank You Lord, most of all
For the ability to know
There is a God in Heaven
And a Home for me to go

Thank You for the voice I have
For which to sing You praise
Thank You for the Holy opportunities
From darkness I was raised

Thank You Lord in Heaven
For blessing me with faith
Thank You for Your Love
Thank You for Your Grace

This love song has no ending
Through eternity it will ring
This, dear Lord is a love song
Written for my Holy King

Amen Amen Amen

God Of Many Names
May These Pages Help Bring Your
Children Home
Amen
Amen
Amen

www.ingramcontent.com/pod-product-compliance
Lightning Source LLC
Chambersburg PA
CBHW051709040426
42446CB00008B/793